DATE DUE

DEMCO 38-296

BY JOSEPH BRODSKY

Elegy for John Donne and Other Poems
Selected Poems
A Part of Speech
Less Than One
To Urania
Marbles
Watermark
On Grief and Reason
So Forth

SO FORTH

JOSEPH

BRODSKY

SO FORTH

[POEMS]

The Noonday Press

Farrar, Straus and Giroux

New York

ıday Press
, Straus and Giroux
'est, New York 10003

Copyright © 1996 by the Estate of Joseph Brodsky
All rights reserved
Distributed in Canada by Douglas & McIntyre Ltd.
Printed in the United States of America
First published in 1996 by Farrar, Straus and Giroux
First Noonday edition, 1998

The Library of Congress has catalogued the hardcover edition as follows:
Brodsky, Joseph.
So forth : poems / Joseph Brodsky.
p.   cm.
ISBN 0-374-26649-2
I. Title.
PS3552.R6229S6   1995
811'.54—dc20   94-24631

"Infinitive," "A Song," "Epitaph for a Centaur," "Exeter
Revisited," "Transatlantic," "Anti-Shenandoah," "Ab Ovo,"
"Törnfallet," "Song of Welcome," "Elegy ('Whether you
fished . . .')," "Kolo," "Anthem," "A Tale," "Ode to Concrete,"
"At the City Dump in Nantucket," "A Postcard," "Reveille,"
"Blues," "At a Lecture," "Love Song," and "To My Daughter"
were written in English.
All the other poems were translated from the Russian by the author,
except the following: "New Life" was translated by David
MacFadyen and the author; "An Admonition" was translated by
George L. Kline and the author; "Axiom," "Homage to Chekhov,"
and "After Us" were translated by Jonathan Aaron and the author;
"Venice: Lido" was translated by Alan Myers; "View from the Hill"
was translated by Alan Myers and the author; and "Cappadocia"
was translated by Paul Graves and the author.

Acknowledgments are made to Antaeus, The New Republic, The
New York Review of Books, The New York Times, Princeton
University Library Chronicle, Queen's Quarterly, The Times
Literary Supplement, and Western Humanities Review, where
some of these poems originally appeared in somewhat different
form. The following poems first appeared in The New Yorker: "A
Song," "New Life," "Angel," "In Memory of My Father: Australia,"
"Porta San Pancrazio," "Transatlantic," "Homage to Girolamo
Marcello," "Ab Ovo," "Portrait of Tragedy," "Törnfallet,"
"Lullaby," and "Homage to Chekhov"—all in slightly different form.

To my wife and to my daughter

Contents

SO FORTH

Infinitive

To Ulf Linde

Dear savages, though I've never mastered your tongue, free of
                                          pronouns and gerunds,
I've learned to bake mackerel wrapped in palm leaves and favor raw
                                          turtle legs,
with their flavor of slowness. Gastronomically, I must admit, these years
since I was washed ashore here have been a non-stop journey,
and in the end I don't know where I am. After all, one keeps carving
                                          notches only
so long as nobody apes one. While you started aping me even before
                                          I spotted
you. Look what you've done to the trees! Though it's flattering to be
                                          regarded
even by you as a god, I, in turn, aped you somewhat, especially with
                                          your maidens
—in part to obscure the past, with its ill-fated ship, but also to cloud
                                          the future,
devoid of a pregnant sail. Islands are cruel enemies
of tenses, except for the present one. And shipwrecks are but flights
                                          from grammar
into pure causality. Look what life without mirrors does
to pronouns, not to mention one's features! Perhaps your ancestors also
ended up on this wonderful beach in a fashion similar
to mine. Hence, your attitude toward me. In your eyes I am
at the very least an island within an island. And anyhow, watching
                                          my every step,

you know that I am not longing for the past participle or the past
                                                    continuous
—well, not any more than for that future perfect of yours deep in
                                          some humid cave,
decked out in dry kelp and feathers. I write this with my index finger
on the wet, glassy sand at sunset, being inspired perhaps
by the view of the palm-tree tops splayed against the platinum sky
                                                    like some
Chinese characters. Though I've never studied the language.
                                  Besides, the breeze
tousles them all too fast for one to make out the message.

                                                    1994

A Song

I wish you were here, dear,
I wish you were here.
I wish you sat on the sofa
and I sat near.
The handkerchief could be yours,
the tear could be mine, chin-bound.
Though it could be, of course,
the other way around.

I wish you were here, dear,
I wish you were here.
I wish we were in my car,
and you'd shift the gear.
We'd find ourselves elsewhere,
on an unknown shore.
Or else we'd repair
to where we've been before.

I wish you were here, dear,
I wish you were here.
I wish I knew no astronomy
when stars appear,
when the moon skims the water
that sighs and shifts in its slumber.
I wish it were still a quarter
to dial your number.

I wish you were here, dear,
in this hemisphere,
as I sit on the porch
sipping a beer.
It's evening, the sun is setting;
boys shout and gulls are crying.
What's the point of forgetting
if it's followed by dying?

1989

A Footnote

to Weather Forecasts

A garden alley with statues of hardened mud,
akin to gnarled, stunted tree trunks.
Some of them I knew personally; the rest
I see for the first time ever. Presumably they are gods
of local woods and streams, guardians of silence.
As for the feminine shapes—nymphs and so forth—they look
thought-like, i.e., unfinished;
each one strives to keep, even here,
in the future that came, her vagrant's status.

A chipmunk won't pop up and cross the path.
No birdsong is audible, nor, moreover, a motor.
The future is a panacea
against anything prone to repetition.
And in the sky there are scattered, like a bachelor's
clothes, clouds, turned inside out
or pressed. It smells of conifer—
this prickly substance of not so familiar places.
Sculptures loom in the twilight, darkening
thanks to their proximity to each other, thanks
to the indifference of the surrounding landscape.

Should any one of them speak, you would
sigh rather than gasp or shudder
upon hearing well-known voices, hearing
something like "The child wasn't yours" or "True,
I testified against him, but out of fear,

not jealousy"—petty, twenty-
odd-year-old secrets of purblind hearts
obsessed with a silly quest for power
over their likes. The best ones among them were
at once the executioners and the victims.

It's good that someone else's memories
interfere with your own. It's good that some
of these figures, to you, appear
alien. Their presence hints
at different events, at a different sort of fate—
perhaps not a better one, yet clearly
the one that you missed. This unshackles
memory more than imagination—
not forever, of course, but for a while. To learn
that you've been deceived, that you've been completely
forgotten, or, the other way around,
that you are still being hated
is extremely unpleasant, but to regard yourself
as the hub of even a negligible universe,
unbearable and indecent.

                              A rare,
perhaps the only, visitor to these parts,
I have, I suppose, a right
to describe the observed. Here it is, our little
Valhalla, our long overgrown estate

in time, with a handful of mortgaged souls,
with its meadows where a sharpened sickle
won't roam, in all likelihood, with abandon,
and where snowflakes float in the air as a good example
of poise in a vacuum.

1986

Star of
the Nativity

In the cold season, in a locality accustomed to heat more than
to cold, to horizontality more than to a mountain,
a child was born in a cave in order to save the world;
it blew as only in deserts in winter it blows, athwart.

To Him, all things seemed enormous: His mother's breast, the steam
out of the ox's nostrils, Caspar, Balthazar, Melchior—the team
of Magi, their presents heaped by the door, ajar.
He was but a dot, and a dot was the star.

Keenly, without blinking, through pallid, stray
clouds, upon the child in the manger, from far away—
from the depth of the universe, from its opposite end—the star
was looking into the cave. And that was the Father's stare.

December 1987

New Life

Imagine that war is over, that peace has resumed its reign.
That you can still make a mirror. That it's a cuckoo
or a magpie, and not a Junkers, that chirps in the twigs again.
That a window frames not a town's rubble but its rococo,
palms, magnolias, pine trees, tenacious ivy, grass,
laurel. That the cast-iron lace the moon used to shepherd
clouds in, in the end endured the onslaught of mimosa, plus
bursts of agave. That life must start from the very threshold.

People exit their rooms, where chairs like the letter *b* or else
h shield them from vertigo on occasion.
They are of use to nobody save themselves,
pavement flagstones, the rules of multiplication.
That's the impact of statues. Of their empty niches, more
accurately. Well, failing sanctity, one still can use its byword.
Imagine that this is all true. Imagine you speak of your-
self while speaking of them, of anything extra, sideward.

Life starts anew indeed like this—with a painted view
of a volcanic eruption, of a dinghy high waves beleaguer.
With the attendant feeling it's only you
who survey the disaster. With the feeling that you are eager
to shift your gaze any moment, catch sight of a couch, a blast
of peonies in a Chinese vase, sallow against the plaster.
Their garish colors, their wilting mouths must
be, in their turn, harbingers of a disaster.

Each thing is vulnerable. The very thought about
a thing gets quickly forgotten. Things are, in truth, the leeches
of thought. Hence their shapes—each one is a brain's cutout—
their attachment to place, their Penelope features;
that is their taste for the future. At sunrise, a rooster's heard.
Stepping out of the tub, wrapped in a bedsheet's linen
in a hotel in the new life, you face the herd
of four-legged furniture, mahogany and cast iron.

Imagine that epics shrink into idylls. That words are but
the converse of flame's long tongues, of that raging sermon
which used to devour your betters greedily like dry wood.
That flame found it difficult to determine
your worth, not to mention warmth. That's why you've survived intact.
That's why you can stomach apathy, that's why you feel fit to mingle
with the pomonae, vertumni, ceres this place is packed
with. That's why on your lips is this shepherd's jingle.

For how long can one justify oneself? However you hide the ace,
the table gets hit with jacks of some odd suit and tailor.
Imagine that the more sincere the voice, the less in it is the trace
of love for no matter what, of anger, of tears, of terror.
Imagine your wireless catching at times your old anthem's hum.
Imagine that here, too, each letter is trailed by a weaning

retinue of its likes, forming blindly now "betsy," now "ibrahim,"
dragging the pen past the limits of alphabet and meaning.

Twilight in the new life. Cicadas that don't relent.
A classicist perspective that lacks a tank or,
barring that, dank fog patches to obfuscate its end;
a bare parquet floor that never sustained a tango.
In the new life, no one begs the moment, "Stay!"
Brought to a standstill, it quickly succumbs to dotage.
And your features, on top of that, are glazed enough anyway
for scratching their matte side with "Hi" and attaching the postage.

The white stuccoed walls of a room are turning more white because
of a glance shot in their direction and boding censure,
steeped not so much in far meadows' morose repose
as in the spectrum's lack of their self-negating tincture.
A thing can be pardoned plenty. Especially where it cones,
where it reaches its end. Ultimately, one's unbound
curiosity about these empty zones,
about these objectless vistas, is what art seems to be all about.

In the new life, a cloud is better than the bright sun. The rain,
akin to self-knowledge, appears perpetual.
On the other hand, an unexpected train

you don't wait for alone on a platform arrives on schedule.
A sail is passing its judgment on the horizon's lie.
The eye tracks the sinking soap, though it's the foam that's famous.
And should anyone ask you "Who are you?" you reply, "Who—I?
I am Nobody," as Ulysses once muttered to Polyphemus.

1988

Angel

A white, pure-cotton angel
till this day hovering in my closet
on a metallic hanger. It's thanks to him
that nothing untoward in all these years
has ever happened to me, or to these very quarters.
A modest radius, one might say, though clearly
delineated. Having been made unlike
ourselves in the image and in the likeness
but incorporeal, angels possess just color
and velocity. The latter explains their being
everywhere. That's why you are still
with me. Wings and shoulder straps can indeed
manage without a proper torso,
shapely limbs, or love per se, and cherish
anonymity, letting the body burgeon
with happiness whose diameter lies somewhere in evergreen
California.

1992

An Admonition

I

Trekking in Asia, spending nights in odd dwellings, in
granaries, cabins, shacks—timber abodes whose thin
squinted windowpanes harness the world—sleep dressed,
wrapped in your sheepskin, and do your best
always to tuck your head into the corner, as
in the corner it's harder—and in darkness at that—to swing an ax
over your heavy, booze-laden gourd
and to chop it off nicely. Square the circle, in short.

I I

Fear broad cheekbones (including the moon's), pockmarked
skin, and prefer blue eyes to brown eyes. Search hard
for the blue ones, especially when the road takes you into the wood,
into its heart. On the whole, as for eyes, one should
watch for their cut. For at your last instant it's
better to stare at that which, though cold, permits
seeing through: ice may crack, yet wallowing in an ice
hole is far better than in honey-like, viscous lies.

I I I

Always pick a house with baby clothes hanging out
in the yard. Deal only with the over-fifty crowd:
a hick at that age knows too much about fate to gain
anything by attempting to bust your brain;
same thing, a squaw. Hide the money in your fur coat's
collar or, if you are traveling light, in your brown culottes

[*16*]

under the knee—but not in your boots, since they'll find the dough
easily there. In Asia, boots are the first to go.

IV

In the mountains, move slowly. If you must creep, then creep.
Magnificent in the distance, meaningless closer up,
mountains are but a surface standing on end. The snail-
like and, it seems, horizontal meandering trail
is, in fact, vertical. Lying flat in the mountains, you
stand. Standing up, you lie flat. Which suggests your true
freedom's in falling down. That's the way, it appears,
to conquer, once in the mountains, vertigo, raptures, fears.

V

If somebody yells "Hey, stranger!" don't answer. Play deaf and dumb.
Even though you may know it, don't speak the tongue.
Try not to stand out—either in profile or
full face; simply don't wash your face at times. What's more,
when they rip a cur's throat with a saw, don't cringe.
Smoking, douse your butts with spittle. And besides, arrange
to wear gray—the hue of the earth—especially underclothes,
to reduce the temptation to blend your flesh with earth.

VI

When you halt in the desert, make an arrow from pebbles, so,
if suddenly woken up, you'll fathom which way to go

in the darkness. At nights, demons in deserts try
travelers' hearts. He who heeds their cry
gets easily disoriented: one step sideways and—well, *c'est tout.*
Ghosts, specters, demons are at home in the desert. You
too will discover that's true when, sand creaking under your sole,
all that remains of you is your soul.

VII

Nobody ever knows anything for a fact.
Gazing ahead at your stooping guide's sturdy back,
think that you gaze at the future and keep your distance (if
that is possible) from him. Since, in principle, life
is itself but a distance between here and there, and
quickening the pace pays only when you discern the sound
behind of those running after you down the path
with lowered heads—be they murderers, thieves, the past.

VIII

In the sour whiff of rugs, in the burnt dung's fume,
prize the indifference of things to being regarded from
afar, and in turn lose your own silhouette, turning, thus,
unattainable to binoculars, gendarmes, mass.
Coughing in a cloud of dust, wading through mud, muck, map—
what difference does it make how you would look close-up?
It's even better if some character with a blade
figures out you are a stranger a bit too late.

IX

Rivers in Asia are longer than elsewhere, more rich
in alluvium—that is, murkier. As you reach
for a mouthful, your cupped fingers ladle silt,
and one who has drunk this water would prefer it spilt.
Never trust its reflection. Crossing it, cross it on
a raft built with no other hands but the pair you own.
Know that the gleam of a campfire, your nightly bliss,
will, by sliding downstream, betray you to enemies.

X

In your letters from these parts don't divulge whom and
what you've seen on your way. If anything should be penned,
use your varying feelings, musings, regrets, et al.:
a letter can be intercepted. And after all,
the movement of a pen across paper is,
in itself, the worsening of the break between you and those
with whom you won't any longer sit or lie down—with whom,
unlike the letter, you won't share—who cares why—a home.

XI

When you stand on an empty stony plateau alone
under the fathomless dome of Asia in whose blueness an airplane
or an angel sometimes whips up its starch or star—
when you shudder at how infinitesimally small you are,
remember: space that appears to need nothing does

crave, as a matter of fact, an outside gaze,
a criterion of emptiness—of its depth and scope.
And it's only you who can do the job.

1986

In Memory of My Father:
Australia

You arose—I dreamt so last night—and left for
Australia. The voice, with a triple echo,
ebbed and flowed, complaining about climate,
grime, that the deal with the flat is stymied,
pity it's not downtown, though near the ocean,
no elevator but the bathtub's indeed an option,
ankles keep swelling. "Looks like I've lost my slippers"
came through rapt yet clear via satellite.
And at once the receiver burst into howling *"Adelaide! Adelaide!"*—
into rattling and crackling, as if a shutter,
ripped off its hinges, were pounding the wall with inhuman power.

Still, better this than the silky powder
canned by the crematorium, than the voucher—
better these snatches of voice, this patchwork
monologue of a recluse trying to play a genie

for the first time since you formed a cloud above a chimney.

1989

So Forth

Summer will end. September will come. Once more it's okay to shoot
duck, woodcock, partridge, quail. "You've grown long in the tooth,"
a belle may sigh, and you'll cock up your double-barrel,
but to inhale more oxygen rather than to imperil
grouse. And the keen lung will twitch at a sudden whiff
of apricots. On the whole, the world changes so fast, as if
indeed at a certain point it began to mainline
some muck obtained from a swarthy alien.

The point, of course, is not autumn. And not one's own features, which
alter like those of an animal approaching the one who'll catch
it. But this feeling of a puny paintbrush left idle
by the painting that lacks a frame, a beginning, an end, a middle.
Not to mention a gallery, not to mention a nail.
And a train in the distance runs whistling along the rail,
though you will spot no smoke inspecting its inventory.
But in a landscape's view, motion is mandatory.

That goes for autumn; that goes for time per se,
like when you quit smoking, or else when the trees you see
ape fanning-out tracks at last freed of their wheels' malfunction
and the edge of the forest echoes a rustling junction.
And it's not a lump but a hedgehog that fills your throat,
for you can't enjoy any longer the silhouette
of a steamship at sea, and an airplane's callous
profile looks odd on high, having lost its halos.

That's what speed's all about. The belle was right. What would
an ancient Roman, had he risen now, recognize? A wood-
pile, the blue yonder, a cloud's texture,
flat water, something in architecture,
but no one by face. That's how some folk still do
travel abroad at times, but, not entitled to
afterlife, scurry back home hiding their eyes in terror.
And not yet settled after the farewell tremor

a hanky still flits in the air. The others who had the luck
of loving something much more than life, knowing all along
that decrepitude is, after all, that after-
life, loom marble-white in the sun getting no tan and often,
partial in their way to history's pleasures, gaze
fixedly at some point in the distance. And the greater the latter's haze,
the more there are points like this defying one's aim and cartridge,
the more speckled turn the eggs of quail, woodcock, grouse, partridge.

1989

Constancy

Constancy is an evolution of one's living quarters into
a thought: a continuation of a parallelogram or a rectangle
by means—as Clausewitz would have put it—
of the voice and, ultimately, the gray matter.
Ah, shrunken to the size of a brain-cell parlor
with a lampshade, an armoire in the "Slavic
Glory" fashion, four studded chairs, a sofa,
a bed, a bedside table with
little medicine bottles left there standing like
a kremlin or, better yet, Manhattan.
To die, to abandon a family, to go away for good,
to change hemispheres, to let new ovals
be painted into the square—the more
volubly will the gray cell insist
on its actual measurements, demanding
daily sacrifice from the new locale,
from the furniture, from the silhouette in a yellow
dress; in the end—from your very self.
A spider revels in shading especially the fifth corner.
Evolution is not a species'
adjustment to a new environment but one's memories'
triumph over reality, the ichthyosaurus pining
for the amoeba, the slack vertebrae of a train

thundering in the darkness, past
the mussel shells, tightly shut for the night, with their
spineless, soggy, pearl-shrouding contents.

1989

Brise Marine

Dear, I ventured out of the house late this evening, merely
for a breath of fresh air from the ocean not far away.
The sun was smoldering low like a Chinese fan in a gallery
and a cloud reared up its huge lid like a Steinway.

A quarter century back you craved curry and dates from Senegal,
tried your voice for the stage, scratched profiles in a sketch pad,
dallied with me—but later alloyed with a chemical
engineer and, judging by letters, grew fairly stupid.

These days you've been seen in churches in the capital and in provinces,
at rites for our friends or acquaintances, now continuous;
yet I am glad, after all, that the world still promises
distances more inconceivable than the one between us.

Understand me correctly, though: your body, your warble, your
                                                    middle name
now stir practically nothing. Not that they've ceased to burgeon;
but to forget one life, a man needs at minimum
one more life. And I've done that portion.

You got lucky as well: where else, save in a snapshot perhaps,
will you forever remain free of wrinkles, lithe, caustic, vivid?
Having bumped into memory, time learns its impotence.
Ebb tide; I smoke in the darkness and inhale rank seaweed.

1989

Centaurs I

They briskly bounce out of the future and having cried "Futile!"
immediately thud back up to its cloud-clad summit.
A branch bends, burdened with birds larger than space—new style,
stuffed not with dawn or feathers but only with "Damn it, damn it."
A horizontal *mare* stained with sunset. A winter evening,
tired of its eye-batting blueness, fondles
like a witless atom on the eve of being
split the remaining hours' golden
chain. A burnt matchstick's residue, a myopic
naked statue, a pergola looming wanly
are excessively real, excessively stereoscopic
since there's nothing they can turn themselves into. Only
horizontal properties, in their fusion, can spawn a monster
with a substantial fallout or follow-
up. For an explosion-sponsored
profile, there is no tomorrow.

Centaurs II

Part ravishing beauty, part sofa, in the vernacular—Sophie,
after hours filling the street whose windows are partly faces
with the clatter of her six heels (after all, a catastrophe
is something that always ogles the guises a lull refuses),
is rushing to a rendezvous. Love consists of tulle, horsehair,
blood, bolsters, cushions, springs, happiness, births galore.
Two-thirds a caring male, one-third a race car—Cary
for short—greets her joyfully with his idling roar
and whisks her off to a theater. Every thigh, from the age of swaddles,
shows the craving of muscles for furniture, for the antics
of mahogany armoires whose panels, in turn, show a subtle
yen for two-thirds, full-face, profiles anxious
for a slap. Whisks her off to a theater in whose murkiness—

                                        perspiring, panting,
running each other over, kneading veneer with tire—
they enjoy off and on a drama about the life of puppets

which is what we were, frankly, in our era.

Centaurs III

A marble-white close-up of the past-*cum*-future hybrid,
cast as a cross between muscular torso and horse's ibid,
or else as a simple grammatical "was" and "will" in
the present continuous. Cast this thing as a million
boring details! in the fairy tale's hut on chicken
feet! Plus, ourselves in its chairs—to cheapen
the sight. Or merged with those whom we loved, or loved to
merge with on horizontal sheets. Or in the nubile auto-
mobile, i.e., as a perspective's captives. Or willy-nilly
in the brain's gray recesses. Cast it out loud, shrilly,
as a thought about death—frequent, tactile, aching.
Cast it as life right now mixed with afterlife where, like eggs in
a string bag, we all are alike and equally petrifying
to the mother hen who, sparing its yolk the frying
pan, flutters up by the means of our era
the six-winged mixture of faith and the stratosphere.

Centaurs IV

The instep-shaped landscape, the shade of a jackboot, with
                                        nothing moving.
The century's serial number matches a rooster's croak.
At dusk, dappled mutanks repair from far fields, a-mooing—
a bulky unicorn flock.
Only the seasons appear to know how to take a hint.
Chasing her slippery soap, a hausfrau sheds a tear
over her man's failure to hold the hilt
of his sword turning into a plowshare.
Still, a framed watercolor depicts a storm;
in a novel, the second letter is the previous one's dead ringer.
Near the cinema youngsters linger
like tightly corked bottles with frozen sperm.
The evening sky offers little to hope for, still less to cope
with. And only a veteran can still recall the foreign
name of a trench that a star has fallen
into, escaping the telescope.

1988

Epitaph for a Centaur

To say that he was unhappy is either to say too much
or too little: depending on who's the audience.
Still, the smell he'd give off was a bit too odious,
and his canter was also quite hard to match.
He said, They meant just a monument, but something went astray:
the womb? the assembly line? the economy?
Or else, the war never happened, they befriended the enemy,
and he was left as it is, presumably to portray
Intransigence, Incompatibility—that sort of thing which proves
not so much one's uniqueness or virtue, but probability.
For years, resembling a cloud, he wandered in olive groves,
marveling at one-leggedness, the mother of immobility.
Learned to lie to himself, and turned it into an art
for want of a better company, also to check his sanity.
And he died fairly young—because his animal part
turned out to be less durable than his humanity.

1988

Axiom

The world was wrought of a mixture of dirt, water, fire,
and air, with the scream "Don't touch me!" embedded in that mire,
rupturing first a plant, eventually a face,
so that you'd never presume the world was a naked place.
Then there rose vast rooms, furniture, ardent loves,
the past's appetite for the future, the tenor's for busted lungs.
Letters broke into motion, making the eyeball roll,
and emptiness grew fearful for its very soul.
Birds were the first to detect this, although a star,
too, signals the fate of a stone that's slung astray.
Any sound, be it music, a whisper, the howling wind,
is the fruit of anything's friction against its kind.
In shrieking beaks, in cumulus, in blazing pulsars none see,
the ear makes out a nagging "No vacancy,"
either an echo of the carpenter's boy or else
addressless stone-cold suns sputtering SOS.
And heeding the shrill "Amscray! Beat it! Vanish! Grab
your junk and get lost!" space itself, alias the backdrop
of life, rendered blind by a surfeit of plots,
heads toward pure time, where no one applauds.
Don't be afraid, though: I've been there. There in its bowels looms
a huge, wrinkle-spinning wheel, its roots
plugged into a raw material whose supply
we, the deposits, eagerly multiply.

1990

North of Delphi

Gedenke meiner,
flüstert der Staub
—Peter Huchel

The plight of a pawn tells the king what it's all about.
A speck of land in the distance—that you are traveling on a boat.
Slight, sated notes in the voice of your sweetheart in the receiver—
that you've got a successor: a surgeon? an engineer?
a student? A junction's veneer—that you're getting nearer,
that the boiled egg won't sport its battered shell forever.

In each one of us sits a peasant, a real ace
at weather forecasting. For instance, leaves falling face
down in autumn mean meager crops. The oracle is no better
when the law in a raincoat crosses your threshold: your
days are numbered—by a jury, or
they are pussycat lacrimae, scarce and bitter.

Say what you will but nature won't rob us of omens, hints.
A cherub might not distinguish his front from his
rear. Not so man. To man, every perspective empties
itself of his silhouette, echo, smell.
Whenever something rings a bell,
it sure rings for him, as they clink, drink, and round up the empties.

So your option is bravery. The palm's tangled lines,
thirteens and, moreover, sixty-nines,
plus the stucco effect in Balthazar's bedchamber
prove only that fate, alas,
has fewer options than victims to find itself at a loss:
you'll end up exactly the way a gypsy foresaw your neighbor,

your sister, your brother, your colleague's wife
—but not you. The pen creaks in a silence that clearly vies
for its posthumous version, for a dance-hall reversal—
it's that deafening! A kind of anti-war.
All that means, however, that you've grown old, that a tired worm
in a beak quits coiling, becomes a morsel.

The dust settles down on objects in summer like winter snow.
This owes to surface, to flatness; essentially to its own
upward pull: toward snow, dust, et cetera; toward blissful
nonexistence. And, as a verse line does,
"Don't forget me," whispers the settled dust
to the hand with the cloth, and the wet cloth absorbs this whisper.

The strength of contempt tells you new times won't wait.
The glare of a star—that pity is rendered void,
as the concession of energy to low temperature
or as a sign that you'd better put
out your lamp, that the pen creaking across the pad
in the limitless silence is bravery in miniature.

Harken then to these words as to the worm's true song
and not to the music of spheres for centuries and so on.
Worse than a bird's tune, it might get a better billing
than the aria of a fish. What's coming no padlock can
check. Yet evil can't happen to an evil man.
It's the fear of tautology that guarantees well-being.

1989

Exeter Revisited

Playing chess on the oil tablecloth at Sparky's
Café, with half & half for whites,
against your specter at noon, two flights
down from that mattress, and seven years later. Scarcely
a gambit, by any standard. The fan's dust-plagued
shamrock still hums in your window—seven
years later and pints of semen
under the bridge—apparently not unplugged.
What does it take to pledge allegiance
to another biography, ocean, creed?
The expiration date on the Indian Deed?
A pair of turtledoves, two young pigeons?
The Atlantic, whose long-brewed invasion looks,
on the beaches of Salisbury, self-defeating?
Or the town hall cupola, still breast-feeding
its pale, cloud-swaddled Lux?

1988

Vertumnus

In memory of Giovanni Buttafava

I

I met you the first time ever in latitudes you'd call foreign.
Your foot never trod that loam; your fame, though, had reached
those quarters
where they fashion the fruit habitually out of plaster.
Knee-deep in snow, you loomed there: white, moreover naked,
in the company of one-legged, equally naked trees,
in your part-time capacity as an expert
on low temperatures. "Roman Deity"
proclaimed a badly faded notice,
and to me you were a deity, since you knew
far more of the past than I (the future
for me in those days was of little import).
On the other hand, apple-cheeked and curly-
haired, you might well have been my agemate; and though you
knew not a word
of the local dialect, somehow we got to talking.
Initially, I did the chatting. Something about Pomona,
our stubbornly aimless rivers, obstinate foul weather,
the absence of greens and money, leapfrogging seasons
—about things, I thought, that should be up your alley
if not in their essence, then in their common pitch
of lament. Little by little (lament is the universal
ur-tongue; most likely, in the beginning
was either "ouch" or "ai") you began to respond: to squint,
to blink, to furrow your brow; then the lower part of your oval

sort of melted, and your lips were slowly set in motion.
"Vertumnus," you squeezed out finally. "I am called Vertumnus."

II

It was a wintry, pallid—more exactly, a hueless day.
The limbs, the shoulders, the torso—as we proceeded
from subject to subject—were gradually turning pinkish,
and were draped with fabric: a shirt, a jacket, trousers,
a moss-colored coat, shoes from Balenciaga.
The weather got warmer also, and you, at times falling still,
would listen intently into the park's soft rustle,
picking up and examining occasionally a gluey leaf
in your search for just the right word, the right expression.
At any rate, if I am not mistaken,
by the time I, now excessively animated,
was holding forth on history, wars, lousy crops,
brutal government, the lilac had already drooped past its bloom,
and you sat on the bench, from a distance looking
like an average citizen, impoverished by the system;
your temperature was ninety-eight point six.
"Let's go," you muttered, touching me on the elbow.
"Let's go. I'll show you the parts where I was born and grew up."

III

The road there led quite naturally through the clouds,
resembling gypsum in color and, later, marble

so much that it crossed my mind that you had in mind precisely
this: washed-out outlines, chaos, the world in ruins—
though this would have signaled the future, while you already
existed. Shortly afterwards, in an empty
café in a drowsy small town fired white-hot by noon,
where someone who dreamt up an arch just couldn't stop more from
                                                    coming,

I realized I was wrong when I heard you chatting
with some local crone. The language turned out to be
a mix of the evergreen rustle and the ever-blue bubbling of
waves, and so rapid that in the course of the conversation,
you several times, in front of my eyes, turned into
her. "Who is she?" I asked when we ventured out.
"She?" You just shrugged your shoulders. "No one. To you, a goddess."

IV

It got a bit cooler. We started to chance more often
upon passersby. Some of them would be nodding,
others looked sideways, becoming thus mere profiles.
All of them, however, were noticeably dark-haired.
Each one behind his back had an impeccable perspective,
not excluding the children. As for old men, in their
cases, it coiled like a shell of some snail or other.
Indeed, the past in these parts was much more abundant
than the present! The centuries outnumbered
cars, parked or passing. People and sculpted figures,
as they drew near and as they receded,

neither grew large nor petered out, thus proving
they were, as it were, invariable magnitudes.
It was strange to observe you in your natural circumstances!
Stranger still was the fact that nearly everybody
understood me. This had to do, perhaps,
with the ideal acoustics, caused by the architecture,
or with your intervention—with the basic penchant of an
absolute ear for garbled sounds.
"Don't be surprised. My field is metamorphosis.
Whomsoever I glance at acquires at once my features.
To you, this may come in handy. You are, after all, abroad."

v

A quarter century later I hear your voice, Vertumnus,
uttering these words, and I sense with my skin the steady
stare of your pearl-gray eyes,
odd in a southerner. In the backdrop there are palm trees,
like Chinese characters tousled by the *tramontana*,
and cypresses like Egyptian obelisks.
Noon; a decrepit balustrade somewhere
in Lombardy; and its sun-splattered mortal visage
of a deity! A provisional one for a
deity, but for me the only
one. With widow's peak, with mustachio
(à la Maupassant more than Nietzsche),
with a much thickened—for the sake of disguise, no doubt—
torso. On the other hand, it is not

for me to flash my diameter, to mimic Saturn,
to flirt with a telescope. Everything leaves a spoor,
time especially. Our rings are
those of fat trees with their prospective stump,
not the ones of a rustic round dance in the dooryard,
let alone of a hug. To touch you is to touch a truly
astronomical sum of cells,
which fate always finds affordable, but to which
only tenderness is proportionate.

VI

And I have ensconced myself in the world where your word and gesture
were imperative. Mimicry, imitation
were regarded as loyalty. I've mastered the art of merging
with the landscape the way one fades into the furniture or the curtains
(which, in the end, influenced my wardrobe).
Now and then in the course of a conversation
the first-person-plural pronoun would start to dribble
off my lips, and my fingers acquired the agility of hedged hawthorn.
Also, I quit glancing back over my padded shoulder. Hearing
footsteps behind me, nowadays I don't tremble:
as previously a chill in my shoulder blades,
nowadays I sense that behind my back also stretches
a street overgrown with colonnades, that at its far end
also shimmer the turquoise crescents
of the Adriatic. Their total is, clearly,

your present, Vertumnus—small change, if you will; some loose
silver with which, occasionally, rich infinity
showers the temporary. Partly out of superstition,
partly, perhaps, because it alone—
the temporary—is capable of sensation,
of happiness. "In this sense, for the likes of me,"
you would squint, "your brethren are useful."

VII

With the passage of years I came almost to the conviction
that the joy of life had become, for you, second nature.
I even started to wonder whether joy is indeed that safe
for a deity. Whether it's not eternity
that a deity pays with in the end for the joy of life.
You'd just brush all this off. But nobody, my Vertumnus,
nobody ever rejoiced so much in the transparent
spurt, in the brick of a basilica, in pine needles,
in wiry handwriting. Much more than we! I even
started to think that you'd gotten infected with
our omnivorousness. Indeed, a view
of a square from a balcony, a clangor of *campanili*,
a streamlined fish, the tattered coloratura
of a bird seen only in profile, laurels'
applause turning into an ovation
—they can be appreciated only by those who do
remember that, come tomorrow, or the day after tomorrow,

all this will end. It's precisely from them, perhaps,
that the immortals learn joy, the knack of smiling
(since the immortals are free from all manner of apprehension).
To the likes of you, in this sense our brethren are useful.

VIII

Nobody ever knew how you were spending nights.
But then that's not strange, taking into consideration
your origins. Once, well past midnight, at the hub of the universe,
I bumped into you, chased by a drove of dimming
stars, and you gave me a wink. Secretiveness? But the cosmos
isn't that secretive. In the cosmos one can see all
things with the naked eye, and they sleep there without blankets.
The intensity of a standard star is such
that its cooling alone can produce an alphabet,
vegetation, sincerity; in the end, ourselves,
with our past, present, future, et cetera—but with the
future especially. We are only
thermometers, brothers and sisters of
ice, not of Betelgeuse. You were made of warmth,
hence your omnipresence. It is difficult to imagine
you in any particular, no matter how shining, dot.
Hence your invisibility. Gods leave no blotches
on a bedsheet, not to mention offspring,
being content with a handmade likeness
in a stony niche, at the end of a garden alley,
happy as a minority; and they are.

IX

An iceberg sails into the tropics. Exhaling smoke, a camel
promotes a pyramid made of concrete, somewhere in the North.
You too, alas, learned to shirk
your immediate duties. To say the least, the four seasons
are more and more one another, eventually getting jumbled
like lire, pounds, dollars, marks, kroner
in a seasoned traveler's wallet.
The papers mutter "greenhouse effect" and "common market,"
but the bones ache at home and overseas alike.
Just look: even that loafer Christo's stone-faced precursor,
which for years used to snake through minefields, is crumbling down.
As a result, birds don't fly away on time
to Africa; characters like myself
less and less often return to the parts they came from;
the rent rises sharply. Apart from having
to exist, one has to pay for that existence monthly.
"The more banal the climate," you once remarked,
"the faster the future becomes the present."

X

On a scorched July dawn, the temperature of a body
plummets, aiming at zero. A horizontal bulk
in the morgue looks like raw material
for garden statuary. Due to a ruptured heart
and immobility. This time around, words
won't do the trick: to you my tongue

[43]

is no longer foreign enough to pay
heed to. Besides, one can't
step twice into the same cloud. Even
if you are a god. Especially, if you are not.

XI

In winter the globe sort of shrinks, mentally flattens out.
The latitudes crawl, in twilight especially, upon one another.
The Alps for them are no obstacle. It smells of an ice age,
it smells, I would add, of neolith and of paleolith;
to use the vernacular, of the future. Since
an ice age is a category of the future, which is
that time when finally one loves no one,
even oneself. When you put on clothes
without planning to drop them off all of a sudden
in somebody's parlor. And when you can't walk out into
the street in your blue shirt alone, not to mention naked.
(I've learned quite a bit from you, but not this.) In a certain sense,
the future's got nobody. In a certain sense,
there is nobody in the future that we'd hold dear.
Of course, there are all those moraines and stalagmites everywhere
looming like louvres and skyscrapers with their meltdown contours.
Of course, something moves there: mammoths, mutant
beetles of pure aluminum, some on skis.
But you were a god of subtropics, with the power of supervision
over mixed forests and the black-earth zone—

[44]

that birthplace of the past. In the future it has no place,
and you've got nothing to do there. So that's why it crawls in winter
on the foothills of the Alps, on the sweet Apennines, snatching
now a small meadow with its clear brook, now something
plain evergreen: a magnolia, a bunch of laurels;
and not only in winter. The future always
arrives when somebody dies. Especially
if it's a man. Moreover, if it's a god.

XII

A dog painted in bright hues of sunrise
barks at the back of a passerby of midnight color.

XIII

In the past those whom you love don't ever
die. In the past they betray you or peter out into a perspective.
In the past the lapels are narrower, the only pair of loafers
steams by a heater like the ruins of boogie-woogie.
In the past a frozen garden bench
with its surplus of slats resembles
an insane equal sign. In the past the wind
to this day animates the mixture
of Cyrillic and Latin in naked branches:
Ж, Ч, Ш, Щ, plus X, Y, Z,
and your laughter is ringing: "As your head honcho said,
there is nothing that matches abracadabra."

XIV

A quarter century later, a streetcar's broken
vertebrae strike a spark in the evening yonder
as a civic salute to a forever darkened
window. One Caravaggio equals two Bernini,
turning either into a cashmere scarf
or a night at the opera. Now these cited
metamorphoses, left apparently unattended,
continue by pure inertia. Other objects, however, harden
in the condition you left them in,
thanks to which, from now on, they can be afforded by
no one. Display of loyalty? Plain predilection for
monumentality? Or is it simply the brazen future
barging in through the doors, and a sellout-resistant soul
acquires before our eyes the status
of a classic, of solid mahogany, of a Fabergé
egg? Most likely, the latter, which is also a metamorphosis,
and to your credit as well.
                              I've got nothing to plait a wreath with
so as to adorn your cold brow in proper fashion
at the closure of this extraordinarily dry year.
In a tastelessly furnished but large apartment,
like a cur that's suddenly lost its shepherd,
I lower myself onto all fours and scratch
the parquet with my claws, as though underneath were hidden—
because it's from down there that wafts the warmth—

your current existence. At the corridor's distant end
dishes are rattling. Under the tightly shut door the frigid
air thickens, rubbed by incessantly rustling dresses.
"Vertumnus," I whisper, pressing my wet cheek hard
against yellow floorboards. "Return, Vertumnus."

1990

Nativity

No matter what went on around them; no matter
what message the snowstorm was straining to utter;
or how crowded they thought that wooden affair;
or that there was nothing for them anywhere;

first, they were together. And—most of all—second,
they now were a threesome. Whatever was reckoned—
the stuff they were brewing, accruing, receiving—
was bound to be split into three, like this evening.

Above their encampment, the sky, cold and idle,
and leaning as big things will do over little,
was burning a star, which from this very instant
had no place to go, save the gaze of the infant.

The campfire flared on its very last ember.
They all were asleep now. The star would resemble
no other, because of its knack, at its nadir,
for taking an alien for its neighbor.

December 1990

Postcard from Lisbon

Monuments to events that never took place: to bloody
but never waged wars; to ardent phrases
swallowed once one's arrested; to a naked body
fused with a conifer, and whose face is
like St. Sebastian's; to aviators
who soared on winged pianos to a cloudy duel;
to the inventor of engines that foiled invaders
using discarded memories for fuel;
to the wives of seafarers bent over one-egged omelettes;
to voluptuous Justice awaiting suitors
and to carnal Respublica; to the comets
that missed this place in their hot pursuit of
infinity—whose features are echoed very
frequently by local vistas (alas, more photo-
genic than habitable); to the discovery
of Infarctica—an unknown quarter
of the afterworld; to the red-tiled seaside
village which dodged the cubist talent
for almost a century; to the suicide
—for unrequited love—of the Tyrant;
to the earthquake greeted by far too many
—say the annals—with cries of "A bargain!";
to the hand which never fondled money,
not to mention a reproductive organ;
to the green leaf choirs' bias against their callous

soloists getting the last ovation;
to happiness; and to dreams which imposed their chaos
on matter, by dint of the population.

1988

August Rain

In broad daylight it starts to get dark with breathless
speed, and a cumulous cloak grows into an uneasy
fur coat off some astral back. An acacia, under the pressure
        of rain, becomes too noisy.
Neither thread nor needle, but something to do with sewing,
almost Singer-made, mixed with a rusty cistern's
spurt, is heard in this chirr, and a geranium bares the sinewed
        vertebrae of a seamstress.

How familial is the rustling of rain! how well it darns and stitches
rents in a worn-out landscape, be that a pasture,
alleyway, puddles, tree-intervals—to foil one's eyesight, which is
        capable of departure
from its range. Rain! vehicle of nearsightedness,
a scribe without his cell, greedy for Lenten fare,
mottling the loamy parchment with his cuneiform brand of silence,
        with his smallpox care.

To turn away from the window! to behold a greatcoat with epaulets
on the brown varnished rack, a red fox on the chair, neglected,
the fringe of a yellow cloth which, having mastered the shibboleths
        of gravity, has resurrected
itself and covered the table where late at night, a threesome,
we sit for supper, and you say in your drowsy, quiet
—almost my own but muted by years' vast distance—
        baritone: What a climate.

1988

Venice: Lido

A rusty Romanian tanker, wallowing out in the azure
like a down-at-heel shoe discarded with sighing pleasure.

The crew, stripped to their pants—womanizers and wankers—
now that they're in the south, sun themselves by the anchors,

without a coin in their pockets to do the city,
which closely resembles a distant pretty

postcard pinned to the sunset; across the water, flocking
clouds, the smell of sweaty armpits, guitars idly plucking.

Ah, the Mediterranean! After your voids, a humble
limb craves a labyrinth, a topographic tangle!

A camel-like superstructure, on its decaying basis,
through binoculars scans the promenade's oasis.

Only by biting the sand, though, all tattoos faded,
can the eye of the needle truly be negotiated

to land at some white table, with a swarthy darling
of local stock, under a floral garland,

and listen as wide-splayed palms, above the bathhouse pennant,
rustle their soiled banknotes, anticipating payment.

1989

Fin de Siècle

The century will soon be over, but sooner it will be me.
That's not the message, though, of a trembling knee.
Rather, the influence of not-to-be

on to-be. Of the hunter upon—so to speak—his fowl,
be that one's heart valve or a red brick wall.
We hear the whiplash's foul

whistle recalling vainly the surnames of those who have loved us back,
writhing in the slippery palms of the local quack.
The world has just lost the knack

of being the place where a sofa, a fox-trot, a lampshade's cream
trimmings, a bodice, a risqué utterance reigned supreme.
Who could foresee time's grim

eraser wiping them off like some chicken scrawl
from a notepad? Nobody, not a soul.
Yet time's shuffling sole

has accomplished just that. Censure it, go ahead.
Now everywhere there are antennae, punks, stumps instead
of trees. No chance of your spotting at

a little café your confreres ruined by kismet, or
at the bar the silk-clad angel who failed to soar
above herself and her whiskey sour

on ice. And all over the place people obscure the view,
now forming a solid mass, now a lengthy queue.
A tyrant's no longer a bugaboo

but a plain mediocrity. Likewise, a car at last
isn't a luxury but the means of extracting dust
out of a street where the cast-

iron leg of a veteran fell silent for good, off course.
And the child is convinced that the wolf is worse
than infantry or the air force.

And somehow your hanky, bypassing your nose more and more
                                                    often, leaps
to your organ of sight, trained on rustling leaves,
taking personally the least

new gap in their emptiness-shielding fence,
the letters *ed* heralding the past tense,
an aria of suspense

sung by a cuckoo's voice. Now it sounds more crude
than, say, Cavaradossi's. Approximately like "Hey, dude,"
or at best like "You should

quit drinking," and your limp palm glides off the decanter's skin,
though it's neither the priest nor the rabbi that's barging in
but the era called "fin

de siècle." Black things are in vogue: camisole, bloomers, hose.
When in the end you relieve your playmate of those
items, your humble house

suddenly gets lit up by something like a twenty-watt.
But instead of an exuberant *"Vivat!"*
the lips drop a flat

"Sorry." New times! Lamentable, sorry times!
Goods in shop windows, sporting nicknames, entice
us into telling the types

of things which are managed easily from the kinds
which we, technologically behind,
now equate to mankind's

ancient quest not so much for something that lets you save
energy as for an inanimate sort of slave;
on the whole, for a safe

anonymity. That's the logical, though unwelcome end
of multiplying, of the demographic trend
whose source is neither the Orient

nor zippers but electricity. The century's winding down. The rush
of time, demanding a ruin, a victim, rejects as trash
Baalbek. And a man won't wash

either. No, give it sentiments! give it ideas, plus
memories. Such is time's, alas,
sweet tooth. Well, I make no fuss

and give. I am not yellow; I am ready to play a thing
of the past, if that's so interesting
to time, eyeing

absentmindedly over its shoulder its measly catch—
which still shows some movement, though not much
else, and is still warm to touch.

I am ready to sink for good in those shifting sands. And I
am prepared that a traveler shambling by
won't focus the beady eye

of his camera on me, and that he won't succumb
to some powerful feeling on my account.
It so happens I can't

stand time that moves on. Time that stands still I still
can stand. Like a solid façade whose style
echoes now a stockpile,

now a chessboard. The century was indeed
not so bad. Well, perhaps the dead
ran a surplus. Yet the living did

that as well. So substantially, in fact,
that presently they could be pickled, packed,
and sealed to attract

stellar customers known for their grand deep-freeze
machinery. Unless, of course, they insist on cheese.
Which could be, with equal ease,

arranged; the holes in the collective memory are the proof.
To the accompaniment of air crashes in not-far-off
spots, the century ends. A prof

mumbles, poking his finger upward, about the atmosphere's
layers, explaining the heat and attendant fears,
but not how one steers

from here to where the cumulous bulky front
is suffused with our "forgive" and "don't
forsake me," which daunt

the ray into changing its gold into some silver roe.
Yet the century, rummaging through its bureau,
treats as retro

even that. Well, small wonder: the more it ticks
and tocks, the busier are young dicks,
the more numerous the antiques

and relics, including the planet, stuck
in its orbit and courting, a sitting duck,
the runaway cul-de-sac

of a comet; including the dog-eared files
of the fallen giants, since every bullet flies
from the future, which plies

its urgent trade with the present and thus needs room
now. Therefore no heirloom
lasts in the dooryard bloom

for long. At the North Pole a husky barks and a flag still twists.
In the West they stare eastward through their clenched fist
making out at least

the barracks, gone suddenly lively. Spooked by the forest of
                                                  hands, birds too
flutter and then take wing rapidly, heading due
south, to its wadis, to

its minarets, turbans, palm trees—and farther down tom-toms roll.
But the longer you scan strange features, the more they gall
you. You conclude that all

over the place the kinship between plain old dirt
and, say, a great painting of the classical sort
lies in that you won't hoard

either's original, ever. That nature, like minstrels of yesteryear
longing for carbons, like a thalamus holding dear
black letters, like a honeybee near

its hive, truly cherishes the mass scale, profuse
outputs, dreading uniqueness for its abuse
of energy, whose

best guardian is licentiousness. Space is fully settled. Time
is welcome to rub against its new surface, I'm
sure, infinitely. All the same,

your eyelid is drooping. Only the seas alone
remain unruffled and blue, telling the dawn "Go on,"
which sounds, from afar, like "gone."

And upon hearing that, one wants to quit one's travail,
shoveling, digging, and board a steamship and sail
and sail, in order to hail

in the end not an island nor an organism Linnaeus never found,
nor the charms of new latitudes, but the other way around:
something of no account.

1989

Porta San Pancrazio

The bees haven't buzzed away, nor has a horseman galloped
off. In the bar Gianicolo, old-timers enjoy their salad
days, and the ice cube melts, cooling the ailing motor
grateful for sipping twice the proverbial water.

Eight years have scurried by. Wars have flared up and smoldered,
families crumbled, scum bared its teeth grown older;
airplanes fell from the sky and the radio mumbled "Jesus."
The linen can still be washed, but the dermal creases

won't yield to the gentlest palm. The sun high above a winter
Rome is jostling the purple smoke with bare rays. The cinder
reeks of burnt leaves, and the fountain is glittering like a wobbly
medal pinned to a cannon at noon for its aimless volley.

Stone is employed worldwide to keep memory captive.
Yet cropping up is much harder than vanishing in a perspective
running out of the city straight through the years and further
in its pursuit of pure time, devoid of love and future.

Life without us is, darling, thinkable. It exists as
honeybees, horsemen, bars, habitués, columns, vistas,
and clouds over this battlefield whose every standing statue
triumphs, with its physique, over a chance to touch you.

1989

[*60*]

Transatlantic

The last twenty years were good for practically everybody
save the dead. But maybe for them as well.
Maybe the Almighty Himself has turned a bit bourgeois
and uses a credit card. For otherwise time's passage
makes no sense. Hence memories, recollections,
values, deportment. One hopes one hasn't
spent one's mother or father or both, or a handful of friends entirely
as they cease to hound one's dreams. One's dreams,
unlike the city, become less populous
the older one gets. That's why the eternal rest
cancels analysis. The last twenty years were good
for practically everybody and constituted
the afterlife for the dead. Its quality could be questioned
but not its duration. The dead, one assumes, would not
mind attaining a homeless status, and sleep in archways
or watch pregnant submarines returning
to their native pen after a worldwide journey
without destroying life on earth, without
even a proper flag to hoist.

1991

View from the Hill

Here is your frozen city cut into marble cubes.
Geometry is bewailing its ravaged quarry.
First, you hear a trio, then a Negro's piano flurry.
The river, as yet unfrozen, still coils and loops,
failing to make the ocean. The meandering urge
is stronger perhaps in a city planned personally by Pollyanna.
Then at the corner flares up an electric birch.
The fat river shines like a black piano.

Once you exit your lair, footsteps ring out behind.
That's the perspective's extra: no murderer keen to follow.
Two years of this place, and yesterday's tomorrow.
And the square, like a record, lets grooves unwind,
an obelisk for spindle. Something took place, that's why.
Say, a century back. Of the triumphant order.
Hence, this oomph of the triumph. Basically, you are small fry.
You are, at best, simply echo fodder.

Snow is falling pell-mell; "cyclone," all sets repeat.
Don't leave the bar, don't leave the bar, stay cozy.
High beams of some automouse make colonnades stampede
madly like Hannibal's elephants, scared and woozy.
There is a stench of desert recalling a widow's laughs.
"Baby, what's wrong?" Sinatra wonders.
Also an echo, though taped. Like the Senate's contours,
blizzard, boredom, low temperature, you, your loves.

Here is your hard-boiled egg, here its nest; here is
its yolk that glows through a shell cracked by the dead of winter.
On the highway, your taxi still overtakes a hearse
loaded with wreaths, apparently rolling in the
same direction as yours, thanks to a comfy rut.
That's the perimeter's spin-off, the call of suburbs,
those stubby districts absorbing, while they sleep, the hubbub
of freight trains, northeasters, fate's gargling throat.

And then—the ocean. An unresponsive tract.
A level expanse, no built-up isthmus.
Where if you are a historian, you've got no business,
nor if you are a doctor, an actor, an architect,
or, moreover, an echo. Since this expanse
lacks a past. All that it hears is the total
of its own waves—that unprecedented tattle
whose volume could be suppressed but once

by Gabriel's trumpet. Here is your splendid set
of horizontal lines. Indeed, the leaf spring
of the cosmos. In which one makes out a lisping
solo by Parker. True; not the pitch you get
from an archangel, judging by the spit it yields.
And beyond that, northbound and getting smaller
in the darkness, now vanishes, now pops up a trawler,
like a church, lost somewhere amid the fields.

1992

Homage to

Girolamo Marcello

Once in winter I, too, sailed in
here from Egypt, believing that I'd be greeted
on the crowded quay by my wife in resplendent furs
and a tiny veiled hat. Yet I was greeted
not by her but by two small, decrepit
Pekinese with gold teeth. Their German owner
told me later that, should he be
robbed, the Pekinese might help him
to make ends meet; well, at least initially.
I was nodding and laughing.

The quay was infinite and completely
vacant. The otherworldly
winter light was turning palazzi into porcelain crockery
and the populace into those who won't
dare to touch it.
Neither veil nor, for that matter, furs
were at issue. The sole transparent
thing was the air and its pinkish laced
curtain in the hotel "Meleager and Atalanta,"
where, as far back as then, eleven years ago,
I could have surmised, I gather,
that the future already
had arrived. When a man's alone,
he's in the future—since it can manage
without the supersonic stuff,
streamlined bodies, an executed tyrant,

crumbling statues; when a man's unhappy,
that's the future.
                    Nowadays I don't get
on all fours any longer in the hotel
room, imitating its furniture and safeguarding
myself against my own maxims. Now to die of grief
would mean, I'm afraid, to die
belatedly, while latecomers
are unwelcome, particularly in the future.

The quay swarms with youngsters chattering in Arabic.
The veil has sprouted into a web of rumors,
dimmed later into a net of wrinkles.
And the Pekinese long ago got consumed by their canine Auschwitz.
No sign of the owner, either. What seems to have survived
is but water and me, since water also
has no past.

1988

Elegy

Sweetheart, losing your looks, go to live in a village.
Mirrors there crave mildew, no maiden's visage.
A river, too, comes with ripples; and fields, in furrows,
clearly forgot for good about stocky fellows.

Nothing but kids around. And as to whose this litter
is, that's known but to those who jail the suckers later,
or to nobody; or to a cobwebbed icon.
And only the law comes to plow in springtime.

Move to a village, sweetheart. A grove or a glebe are where
it's simpler to ponder humus, or what to wear.
There for a hundred miles yours is the only lipstick,
though its slug will do better with no ballistics.

You know, it's better to age where a milepost is nodding,
where beauty means absolutely nothing,
or it means not youthfulness, bosom, semen
—since time, on the whole, is indeed all seasons.

That should cure ennui, though one would be loath to patent
this. And the woods there clamor that everything has happened
already; and not just once. And the total number
of what happened already is the root of their constant clamor.

It's better to age in a village. There, even though a recluse,
you'd easily spot a tiny crucifix in a reckless

stark-naked birch, in a shepherd's purse, in manly
burdocks, in moths aflutter for twenty-four hours only.

And I'll come to join you there. Still, in this ardent cry of
joining you read not your but those beings' triumph,
since, like a bedsheet, earth better follows
not the parlance of love but that of ruts, gulches, hollows.

And even if I won't come! Any sinkhole or crater,
or some dark well's razor-blade-tasting water,
road-shoulder brambles, a hobbling scarecrow
is, frankly, me: that is, what you don't care for.

Go to a village, sweetheart. You know, a ruined
face only proves there exist more fluent
ways of tying the knot—ah, many other methods!
Yet we seldom see what is staring at us.

You know, a landscape is what you never
know. Think of that when you think it's over.
Squinting one day at some colorless brushstrokes, dear,
you'll make out yourself, and a colorless brushstroke near.

1992

Anti-Shenandoah:

Two Skits and a Chorus

I. DEPARTURE

"Why don't we board a train and go off to Persia?
Persia doesn't exist, obviously, but inertia
does. It's a better vehicle than any old engine, Johnny,
and we may have a comfortable, an eventful journey."

"Why do you call me Johnny when you know I am Billy, Mary?
Perhaps because of inertia? It's Johnny you want to marry,
not me. But he is not in Persia, he went off to Warsaw,
although after 1945 it's a different city also."

"Of course, you are Billy, Billy; and I'm not Mary, either.
Actually, I am Suzy: you are welcome to check my Visa.
But let's be Mary and Johnny, like in the Ark of Noah,
or nameless, the way we were when we were spermatozoa."

"Because there are but two sexes, there is a lot of nuance,
and history's where our exes join kings and ruins.
When someone's whereabouts become a mystery,
you should take the train of thought that goes to history."

"Ah, there is so much action! In history, willy-nilly,
Mary becomes just Suzy, and Johnny Billy,
B.C. becomes A.D., and Persia Warsaw.
For history breeds inertia, and vice versa."

"Ah, mixing inertia with history bespeaks individuality!
  Mary, let's take a chance, this father of causality:
  let's take the express to where folks live in utter penury
  and where the reality quickly becomes a memory."

"Oh, he is my dear boy, my slowly peeled banana!"
"And she is my sweetheart filled with Tampax Americana!"
"The future arrives on time whistling *Domine Gloria*,
  and we must take it eastward, where it's always earlier."

II. ARRIVAL

"What is this place? It looks kind of raw.
  The trees stand as if they are about to draw,
  their rustle is so menacing. They, no doubt,
  have seen too many movies—but were they dubbed?"

"I don't mind the place, but who are these guys?
  Is this their true appearance, or disguise?
  They all sell shoelaces but wear no shoes.
  Can we explain to them that we are not Jews?"

"I never knew that history is so much
  inhabited and curious, and prone to touch.
  Oh, do they have a leader? A shah? A khan?
  Frankly, I regret I don't have my gun."

"But I've read many people can't wish the same
  wish. Unless, of course, they are insane.
  I think we are quite safe; they don't want to kill,
  though frankly I regret I am off the pill."

"Ah, this is the past, and it's rather vast,
  and in the land of the cause its effects go bust
  or else get outnumbered in more ways than one:
  we've brought them all the future, and we are left with none."

"One shouldn't speak for others when things get tight.
  You might not have the future, but I just might.
  The future is derivative; they may crack skulls,
  but because they've been so primitive, we've had Pascals."

"So it's goodbye, dear Mary. Hope all goes well.
  We'll meet not in the future but, say, in hell."
"Oh, that would be nice, dear Johnny, that would be great.
  But the afterlife in history occurs quite late."

III. CHORUS
Here they are, for all to see,
  the fruits of complacency.
Beware of love, of A.D., B.C.,
  and the travel agency.

[70]

A train may move fast, but time is slow.
    History's closer
to the Big Bang than to Roman law,
    and you are the loser.

So, our advice to you is, Stay put
    if you can help it.
Always be ready to say Kaput,
    but wear a helmet.

1992

Daedalus in Sicily

All his life he was building something, inventing something.
Now, for a Cretan queen, an artificial heifer,
so as to cuckold the king. Then a labyrinth, this time for
the king himself, to hide from bewildered glances
an unbearable offspring. Or a flying contraption, when
the king figured out in the end who it was at his court
who was keeping himself so busy with new commissions.
The son on that journey perished falling into the sea,
like Phaeton, who, they say, also spurned his father's
orders. Here, in Sicily, stiff on its scorching sand,
sits a very old man, capable of transporting
himself through the air, if robbed of other means of passage.
All his life he was building something, inventing something.
All his life from those clever constructions, from those inventions,
he had to flee. As though inventions
and constructions are anxious to rid themselves of their blueprints
like children ashamed of their parents. Presumably, that's the fear
of replication. Waves are running onto the sand;
behind, shine the tusks of the local mountains.
Yet he had already invented, when he was young, the seesaw,
using the strong resemblance between motion and stasis.
The old man bends down, ties to his brittle ankle
(so as not to get lost) a lengthy thread,
straightens up with a grunt, and heads out for Hades.

1993

Clouds

Ah, summer clouds
of the Baltic! I swear
you are nowhere
to be outclassed.

Isn't your free state
the afterworld's border—
stallions, a warrior,
sometimes a saint?

The Almighty alone
glimpses by lightning
your crumbling lining,
fraying cretonne.

Hence, I, an old
hand at premonitions,
take your omniscience
for non-being's mold,

afterlife's mask.
Steadily running
over the granite,
over the most

humble of seas,
you are the limpid

sculptures of limit-
less genesis.

Cupolas, peaks,
profile of Tolstoy,
muscular torso,
bachelor digs,

candlesticks' vain
meltdown, or Hapsburg
Vienna, an iceberg-
alias-brain,

Eden's debris.
Ah, save the northeaster,
you wouldn't master
geometry!

Your cirric ploys
or cumulous domus
make both the nomads
and the settled rejoice.

Thanks to your reams,
patches, and tatters,
words that one utters
equal one's dreams.

It's you who let
me with your nimbus
trust not in numbers
but in the complete

spurning of weights
and measures in favor
—once and forever—
of phantoms and grace.

It was you, too,
who made the salient
planet an island
paltry for two.

Ah, your rent-free
castles! Those lofty
soft hotbeds of the
heart's tyranny!

Frothy cascades
of seraphs and ball gowns;
crashing of bogus
starched barricades;

conjugal bouts
of butterflies and

the Himalayan
glaciers—ah, clouds,

high in pristine
skies of the Baltic!
Whose stern and vatic
calls have you been

heeding? To whose
might do you yield? Or
who is your builder?
Your Sisyphus?

Who, having found
shapes to your grandeur,
made it surrender
sound? For sound-

less is your great
miracle! Heavy
or scattered, your bevy,
cohort, parade

silently hedge
toward some finish
line, where you'll vanish
—toward the edge

etched by your shoal
that charged it more boldly,
and was lighter than body,
better than soul.

1989

Cappadocia

A hundred and forty thousand warriors of Mithridates Ponticus—
cavalry, archers, armor, swords, lances, helmets, shields—
cross into a foreign territory which is called Cappadocia.
The army has stretched for miles. Horsemen cast gloomy, ominous
glances around. The space, ashamed of its bareness, feels
that, with their every step, the far-off turns cautiously
into the nearby. Especially in the mountains, whose
summits, equally tired of purple
at dawn, of lilac at twilight, of clouds' burnous,
gain, because of the strangers' keensightedness, in their marble
sharpness, if not in distinctness. The army looks
from afar like a river snaking among the rocks,
whose source does its best not to fall too far behind its mouth,
which, in turn, glances back now and then at its lagging source.
And the farther the troops move eastward, the more this sparse
terrain, as though facing a mirror, from a muddy, forsaken chaos

turns, temporarily, into an impassive, sublime backdrop
of history. Shuffling of many feet,
cursing, clinking of harnesses, of stirrups against the sheath,
hubbub, a thicket of spears. Suddenly, with an abrupt
cry, the outrider freezes; is it a phantom, or . . . ?
In the distance, replacing the landscape, across the whole plateau
stand the legions of Sulla. Sulla, forgetting Marius,
brought here legions to clarify to whom,
despite the brand of the winter moon,
Cappadocia belongs. Having come to a halt, the army is

[78]

settling now for a battle. The stony, wide
plateau for the last time looks like a place where no one died.
Sparks of bonfire, bursts of laughter, of singing "The fox was crafty."
Stretched on the naked stone, King Mithridates' hefty
bulk is beholding a dream's perennial milky breast,
hamstrings, wet ringlets, smooth thighs, the torso.

The same is beheld by the rest of his troops, and also
by the legions of Sulla. Which proves, at least,
not the absence of choice but the fullness of moon. In Asia
space tends to hide from itself, and the frequent charge
of monotony, in its conqueror; by and large
in his head, his armor, his beard, which, to make things easier,
it shrouds with the moonlight. Under this silver shroud,
the troops are no longer a river proud
of its length but a sizable lake, whose depth, apparently,
is exactly what space, living here in seclusion, needs,
since that depth is proportionate to those many covered leagues.
That's why often the Parthians, sometimes the Romans (currently
both of them), wander into Cappadocia. Armies are
essentially water, without which neither plateaus nor a
mountain would know how they look in profile, much less

en face. Two sleeping lakes, with the same floating piece of flesh
inside, glow at night like the triumph of flora over
fauna, aiming to coalesce at dawn,
in a ravine, into one common mirror quite fit to own

Cappadocia's all: boulders, lizards, skies—save the oval
of one's face. Only, perhaps, a big
eagle up there in the dark, used to its wing and beak,
knows what lies in the future. Glancing below with utter
apathy, common in birds, since, unlike a king,
a bird is repeatable, an eagle soaring
in the present soars naturally in the future
and of course in the past: in history; in its late-
running show, in its friction—the way it's sounding—
of something temporary against something
permanent, the way matches grate

sandpaper, a dream the reality, troops a terrain. In Asia
daybreaks are rapid. Something chirps. As soon
as you rise, a shiver runs down your spine
infecting with chilliness the stubborn, earth-hugging, drowsy,
long-legged shadows. The milky haze
of dawn, with its coughing, neighing, half-yawn, half-phrase,
rattling of armor, commands to rise.
And, witnessed by half a million eyes,
the sun sets in motion limbs, spears, all manner of sharpened metal,
horsemen, foot soldiers, archers, chariots. Helmets shine,
and the troops march toward each other like line after line
of a book slamming shut in the very middle;
like, more aptly, two mirrors, two shields; like two
faces, two parts of addition, instead of *summa*

resulting in difference and subtracting Sulla
from Cappadocia. Whose grass—which, too,

never knew what it looks like—gains more than anyone
from the screams, the clangor, the noise, the gore
of this smashing and crashing, as its green eyes pore
over the smithereens of a shattered legion
and the fallen Parthians. Waving widely his sharp sword, King
Mithridates, not thinking of anything,
rides ahead amid chaos, crossed weapons, babel.
The battle looks from afar like—"aaagh" carved in stone;
or else like a mirror's silver gone
berserk facing its shiny double.
And with each body falling next, from the ranks, onto this stony glade
the terrain, akin to a dulling blade,
loses its sharpness, gets blurred in the south and mossier
in the east; the silhouette seems to resume its fair
reign. That's how the fallen take into the next world their
trophy: the features of nobody's Cappadocia.

1992

Ab Ovo

Ultimately, there should be a language
in which the word "egg" is reduced to O
entirely. The Italian comes the closest,
naturally, with its *uova*. That's why Alighieri thought
it the healthiest food, sharing the predilection
with sopranos and tenors whose pear-like torsos
in the final analysis embody "opera."
The same pertains to the truly Romantic, that is,
German poets, with practically every line
starting the way they'd begin a breakfast,
or to the equally cocky mathematicians
brooding over their regularly laid infinity,
whose immaculate zeros won't ever hatch.

1996

Via Funari

Ugly gargoyles peek out of your well-lit window,
the Gaetani palace exhales turpentine and varnish,
and Gino's, where the coffee was good and I used to pick up the keys,
has vanished. In Gino's stead
came a boutique; it sells socks and neckties,
more indispensable than either him or us
—from any standpoint, actually. And you are far off in Tunisia
or in Libya, contemplating the lining of
the waves whose lace keeps adorning the Italian coastline:
an homage to Septimus Severus? I doubt whether all this should
be blamed on money, or the passage of time, or me.
In any case, it's no less probable
that the famous inanimateness
of the cosmos, tired of its pretty vicious
infinitude, seeks for itself an earthly
abode; and we come in handy. And, frankly, one should be grateful
when it confines itself to an apartment,
some facial expression, a few brain cells,
and doesn't drive us directly under,
the way it did parents, your kid brother and sister, G.
The doorbell button is but a crater
in miniature, modestly gaping in the
wake of some cosmic touch, the crumb of a meteorite;
all doorways are peppered with this otherworldly smallpox.
Well, we've failed to connect. I think the next opportunity
won't arise very soon. Probably not at all.

Don't regret this, however. I don't believe I could
reveal to you more than Sirius to Canopus,
though it's precisely here, on your doorstep, where
they bump into one another, in broad daylight,
and not in the vigilant, telescope-hugging nighttime.

1995

Portrait of Tragedy

Let's look at the face of tragedy. Let's see its creases,
its aquiline profile, its masculine jawbone. Let's hear its rhesus
contralto with its diabolic rises:
the aria of effect beats cause's wheezes.
How are you, tragedy? We haven't seen you lately.
Hello, the medal's flip side gone lazy.
Let's examine your aspects, lady.

Let's look into her eyes. Into her wide-with-senseless-
pain hazel pupils aimed like lenses
at us in the stalls, or touring in someone else's
predicament, on false pretenses.
Welcome, tragedy, with gods and heroes,
with the curtain exposing your feet, dirty with other eras,
with proper names sunk in the maddening chorus.

Let's put our fingers into her mouth that gnashes
scurvy-eaten keyboards inflamed by wolfram flashes
showing her spit-rich palate with blizzards of kinfolk's ashes.
Let's yank her hem, see if she blushes.
Well, tragedy, if you want, surprise us.
Show us a body betrayed or its demise, devices
for lost innocence, inner crisis.

Ah, but to press ourselves against her cheek, her Gorgon
coiling hairdo! Against the golden
icon's coarse wooden backside that hoards the burden

of proof the better the more her horizons broaden.
Greetings, tragedy, dressed slightly out of fashion,
with lengthy sentences making time look ashen.
Though you feel fine alfresco, it's the morgue you've got a crush on.

Let's tumble into her arms with a lecher's ardor!
Let's drown in her flabby rubble; yes, let's go under.
Let's burrow through her and make mattress fodder.
Who knows, she may carry. A race always needs a founder.
What's new on the schedule, tragedy, in your cartridge?
And re stuffing wombs, what takes more courage
to star in: a scene of carnage or a pile of garbage?

Ah, to inhale her stench of armpits and feces
mixed with the incense clouding subtracted faces;
to exclaim hysterically, You save this
for the sissies! And throw up into her laces.
Thanks, tragedy, for your attempts to cheer up
(since there is no abortion without a cherub),
for jackboots kicking the groin as though it's a stirrup.

Her face is abominable! It's never hidden
by the domino, makeup, duckweed, by heathen
ignorance, or by a fishnet mitten
involved in a stormy ovation, completely smitten.
Thanks, tragedy, for playing decent.

For being direct like a bullet, albeit distant.
For not wasting time, for happening in an instant.

Who are we, after all, neither oils nor statues,
not to allow the mangling of our lives as much as
one wishes? Which, too, could be seen as a boon. The catch is,
a thing must become unpalpable to look matchless.
Don't spurn that, tragedy, the genre of martyrs!
How about the loss of all that's sacred to us for starters?
Small wonder that togas become you as much as tatters.

Look at her, she is scowling! She says, "Good evening,
let me begin. In this business, folks, the beginning
matters more than the end. Give me a human being
and I'll begin with misfortune, so set the wristwatch for grieving."
Go ahead, tragedy! Among our vowels,
pick out the *yi*, born in the Mongol bowels,
and turn it, ripping our gushing ovals,

into a noun, a verb, an adjective! *yi*, our common gargle!
yi, we barf out as our gains and our losses ogle
us, or as we storm the exit. But there, an ogre,
you're looming large with your oblong cudgel and bulging goggle!
Tragedy, hit us like a relative. Make clowns of us.
Knead us into a pulp on our bunks and sofas.
Spit into our souls till you find a surface,

and afterwards also! Make it a swamp, and stir it,
so that neither the Father and Son nor the Holy Spirit
will clear it up. Curdle it into the serried
rubble. Plant there aspens, shoot up acid, and leave needles buried.
Let soul be like nature, tragedy; that won't wear badly.
Let's graft a seraph to the night-work buggy.
As the fruit told the botanist, Fine, make me ugly.

Once you were, dear, a beauty, a power, a non-stop torrent.
You'd come after midnight and flash a warrant.
You were quoting Racine; obscene you weren't.
Now you are the perspective stewed in the dead end. A worried
herd, though, finds its address, and a lamb an oven
by spotting your footprint that's fresh and cloven.
Come on! Fly the gates of your pigsty open.

1991

Yi: the Cyrillic letter **ы**.

Törnfallet

There is a meadow in Sweden
where I lie smitten,
eyes stained with clouds'
white ins and outs.

And about that meadow
roams my widow
plaiting a clover
wreath for her lover.

I took her in marriage
in a granite parish.
The snow lent her whiteness,
a pine was a witness.

She'd swim in the oval
lake whose opal
mirror, framed by bracken,
felt happy broken.

And at night the stubborn
sun of her auburn
hair shone from my pillow
at post and pillar.

Now in the distance
I hear her descant.

She sings "Blue Swallow,"
but I can't follow.

The evening shadow
robs the meadow
of width and color.
It's getting colder.

As I lie dying
here, I'm eyeing
stars. Here's Venus;
no one between us.

1990/1993

Persian Arrow

To Véronique Schiltz

Your wooden shaft has vanished; so has the body
which you clearly missed way back in zero
B.C. Nonetheless, oxidized and badly
chipped, you have reached me, dear devotee of Zeno.

Clockworks tick on. Yet, to put it archly,
they are, like a corked liquid, settled
and immobile. While you are starkly
mobile, heedless of any second.

Could you really guess what lay ahead when bidding
farewell to your string? What grand hiatus
you embarked on, snapping the bow and hitting
the blue yonder the other side of the Euphrates?

Even now, resting in my warm fingers
on a cold afternoon, in an alien chamber,
resembling, thanks to your greenish pigment,
a bay leaf that has outlived its chowder,

you are rushing away, target-free, defiant.
There is no way to catch up with you in a desert; also
in the jungle-like present. For every warmth is finite.
That of the human hand is more so.

1993

Song of Welcome

Here's your mom, here's your dad.
Welcome to being their flesh and blood.
Why do you look so sad?

Here's your food, here's your drink.
Also some thoughts, if you care to think.
Welcome to everything.

Here's your practically clean slate.
Welcome to it, though it's kind of late.
Welcome at any rate.

•

Here's your paycheck, here's your rent.
Money is nature's fifth element.
Welcome to every cent.

Here's your swarm and your huge beehive.
Welcome to the place with its roughly five
billion like you alive.

Welcome to the phone book that stars your name.
Digits are democracy's secret aim.
Welcome to your claim to fame.

•

Here's your marriage, and here's divorce.
Now that's the order you can't reverse.
Welcome to it; up yours.

Here's your blade, here's your wrist.
Welcome to playing your own terrorist;
call it your Middle East.

Here's your mirror, your dental gleam.
Here's an octopus in your dream.
Why do you try to scream?

●

Here's your corncob, your TV set.
Your candidate suffering an upset.
Welcome to what he said.

Here's your porch, see the cars pass by.
Here's your shitting dog's guilty eye.
Welcome to its alibi.

Here are your cicadas, then a chickadee,
the bulb's dry tear in your lemon tea.
Welcome to infinity.

●

Here are your pills on the plastic tray,
your disappointing, crisp X-ray.
You are welcome to pray.

Here's your cemetery, a well-kept glen.
Welcome to a voice that says "Amen."
The end of the rope, old man.

Here's your will, and here's a few
takers. Here's an empty pew.
Here's life after you.

And here are your stars which appear still keen
on shining as though you had never been.
They might have a point, old bean.

Here's your afterlife, with no trace
of you, especially of your face.
Welcome, and call it space.

Welcome to where one cannot breathe.
This way, space resembles what's underneath,
and Saturn holds the wreath.

1992

Elegy

Whether you fished me bravely out of the Pacific
or I pried your shell wide open by the Atlantic
now matters little. A different kind of ocean
erodes nowadays what seemed fairly rocky
and presumably insinuates itself
into your hairdo as well—obliterating
as much as conquering. And, as the poet said,
thou art far in humanity, what with your offspring now
breaking new hearts and balls across this continent,
which is what, I hope, we still have in common.
Still, they are only half you. In a court of law
the inheritance of your mesmerizing beauty
that I thought immortal will be awarded
to nobody, including yourself. For although the gods or genes
are generous lending their properties—say, for a trial run
in these precincts—ultimately they are selfish;
at any rate, they are more vain than you,
having eternity. Which is a far cry from
yet another rented abode in a snowbound village
somewhere up north, where perhaps at this
very moment you stare at your flimsy mirror
returning you surely less than my equally one-dimensional
memory, though to you this makes indeed no difference.

1995

Kolo

In march the soldiers
with rifles on their shoulders.
Out run through brambles
the locals with their bundles.

Off fly the envoys
contemplating new ways
of creating symmetry
in a future cemetery.

Up go the pundits
explicating bandits.
Clearly outworded,
down go the murdered.

The expensive warriors,
sailing by on carriers
flying Old Glory,
signal hunky-dory.

Far is the neighbor,
loveless or unable,
neutral or bullied.
Near is a bullet.

Deep dig new hermits
sporting blue helmets.
Reasonable offers
manufacture orphans.

Blood as a liquid
shows no spilling limit;
one might build finally
here a refinery.

Home stay the virtuous
with their right to watch this
live, while they are dining:
it's a mealtime dying.

Soiled turns the fabric
of the great republic.
Ethics by a ballot
is what it's all about.

Mourn the slaughtered.
Pray for those squatted
in some concrete lair
facing betrayal.

1995

Lullaby

Birth I gave you in a desert
not by chance,
for no king would ever hazard
its expanse.

Seeking you in it, I figure,
won't be wise
since its winter cold is bigger
than its size.

As you suck my breast, this vastness,
all this width,
feeds your gaze the human absence
it's filled with.

Grow accustomed to the desert
as to fate,
lest you find it omnipresent
much too late.

Some get toys, in piles and layers,
wrapped or bound.
You, my baby, have to play with
all the sand.

See that star, at terrifying
height, aglow?

Say, this void just helps it, eyeing
you below.

Grow accustomed to the desert.
Uniform
underfoot, for all it isn't,
it's most firm.

In it, fate rejects a phantom
faint or gross:
one can tell for miles a mountain
by a cross.

Paths one sees here are not really
human paths
but the centuries' which freely
through it pass.

Grow accustomed to the desert:
flesh is not—
as the speck would sigh, wind-pestered—
all you've got.

Keep this secret, child, for later.
That, I guess,
may just help you in a greater
emptiness.

Which is like this one, just ever-
lasting; and
in it love for you shows where
it might end.

Grow accustomed to the desert
and the star
pouring down its incandescent
rays, which are

just a lamp to guide the treasured
child who's late,
lit by someone whom that desert
taught to wait.

December 1992

Homage to Chekhov

Sunset clings to the samovar, abandoning the veranda,
but the tea has gone cold, or is finished; a fly scales a saucer's *dolce*.
And her heavy chignon makes Varvara Andreevna look grander
than ever. Her starched cotton blouse is staunchly
buttoned up to her chin. Vialtsev, deep in his chair, is nodding
over the rustling weekly with Dubrovo's latest swing
at the Cabinet. Varvara Andreevna under her skirts wears not a
thing.

The drawing room's dark piano responds to a dry ovation
of hawthorns. The student Maximov's few random chords
stir the garden's cicadas. In the platinum sky, athwart,
squadrons of ducks, foreshadowing aviation,
drift toward Germany. Hiding in the unlit
library, Dunia devours Nikki's letter, so full of cavils.
No looker; but, boy, what anatomy! And so unlike
hardcovers.

That is why Erlich winces, called in by Kartashov
to join Prigozhin, the doctor, and him at cards. "With pleasure."
Ah, but swatting a fly is simpler than staving off
a reverie of your niece, naked upon the leather
couch and fighting mosquitoes, fighting heat—but to no avail.
Prigozhin deals as he eats: with his belly virtually
crushing the flimsy table. Can the doctor be asked about this little boil?
Perhaps eventually.

Oppressive midsummer twilight; a truly myopic part
of day, when each shape and form loses resolve, gets eerily
vague. "In your linen suit, Piotr Lvovich, it's not so hard
to take you for one of the statues down in the alley." "Really?"
Erlich feigns embarrassment, rubbing his pince-nez's rim.
It's true, though: the far-off in twilight looks near, the near, alien;
and Erlich tries to recall how often he had Natalia
Fiodorovna in his dream.

But does Varvara Andreevna love the doctor? Gnarled poplars crowd
the dacha's wide-open windows with peasant-like abandon.
They are the ones to be asked: their branches, their crow-filled crowns.
Particularly, the elm climbing into Varvara's bedroom:
it alone sees the hostess with just her stockings on.
Outside, Dunia calls for a swim in the night lake: "Come, lazies!"
To leap! overturning the tables! Hard, though, if you are the one
with aces.

And the cicada chorus, with the strength of the stars' display,
burgeons over the garden, sounding like their utterance.
Which is, perhaps, the case. Where am I, anyway?
wonders Erlich, undoing his braces at the outhouse entrance.
It's twenty versts to the railroad. A rooster attempts its *lied*.
The student Maximov's pet word, interestingly, is "fallacy."
In the provinces, too, nobody's getting laid,
as throughout the galaxy.

1993

Ischia in October

To Fausto Malcovati

Once a volcano here belched with zest.
Later, a pelican plucked its breast.
Virgil dwelt not too far away,
and Wystan Auden held drinks at bay.

These days, the palaces' stucco peels,
frightful prices make longer bills.
Yet I somehow still make, amid
all these changes, my line ends meet.

A fisherman sails into the azure,
away from the drying bed linen's lure.
And autumn splashes the mountain ridge
with a wave unknown to the empty beach.

On the balustrade, my wife and child
peer at a distant piano lid
of sail, or at the small balloon
of Angelus fleeing the afternoon.

Unreachable, as it were, by foot,
an island as a kind of fate
suits solely the sirocco; but
we also are fluent at

banging the shutters. A sudden draft
scattering papers right and left

is proof that in this limestone
place we are not alone.

The rectangular, mortar-held eggshell,
enduring the wind's solid brow, as well
as the breakers' wet hammer works,
reveals at dusk three yolks.

The bougainvillea's tightly wound
scrawl helps the isolated ground
to shade its limited shame a bit,
avenging thus space with writ.

Almost no people; so that pronouns
sharpen one's features all at once,
as though speech makes them definite like a lens
at the vista's expense.

And should someone sigh longingly "Home," your hand
more willingly than to the continent
might point to the cumulous peaks where great
worlds rise and disintegrate.

We are a threesome here and I bet
what we together are looking at
is three times more addressless and more blue
than what Aeneas saw sailing through.

1993

Anthem

Praised be the climate
for putting a limit,
after a fashion,
to time in motion.

Of all prisons
the Four Seasons
has the best diet
and welcomes riot.

Asked for its origin
a climate cites oxygen,
but gives no reasons
for its omnipresence.

Detached like Confucius,
hardly conscious,
it may not love us,
but murmurs, "Always."

Being finite,
we certainly find it
promising and heartwarming,
though it's a warning.

A climate's permanence
is caused by the prevalence

of nothingness in its texture
and atmospheric pressure.

Hence, the barometer,
with its Byronic air,
should be, I reckon,
our only icon.

Since the accuracy of mercury
beats that of memory
(which is also mortal),
climate is moral.

When it exhibits
its bad habits,
it blames not parents
but ocean currents.

Or charged with the tedium
and meaninglessness of its idiom,
it won't seek legal
aid and goes local.

Keen on history,
it's also well versed in the mystery
of the hereafter
and looks like their author.

What I have in common
with the ancient Roman
is not a Caesar,
but the weather.

Likewise, the main features
I share with the future's
mutants are those curious
shapes of cumulus.

Praised be the entity
incapable of enmity
and likewise finicky
when it comes to affinity.

Yet if one aspect
of this highly abstract
thing is its gratitude
for finding latitude,

then a rational anthem
sung by one atom
to the rest of matter
should please the latter.

1995

In Front of
Casa Marcello

The sun's setting, and the corner bar bangs its shutters.
Lampposts flare up, as though an actress

paints her eyelids dark violet, looking both rum and scary.
And the headache is parachuting squarely

behind enemy wrinkles. While five enormous
pigeons on the Palazzo Minelli's cornice

are copulating in the last rays of sunset,
paying no heed, as our Stone Age ancest-

ors did, no doubt, to their scruffy neighbors,
already asleep or a little nervous.

The booming bells of the slant bell tower
rooted in the ultramarine sky over

this town are like fruits keen on falling rather
than hitting the ground. If there is another

life, someone picks them up there. Well, pretty
soon we'll find out. Here, where plenty

of saliva, rapturous tears, and even
seed has been shed, in a nook of the earthly Eden,

I stand in the evening, absorbing slowly
with the dirty sponge of my lungs the lovely,

transparent, autumn-*cum*-winter, lucent
local oxygen, pink with loosened

tiles and a windowsill's carnation,
and giving the scent of cells' liberation

from time. The money-like, crumpled water
of the canal, buying off the palazzo's outer

riches, ends up with a somewhat shady,
peeling-off deal that includes a shaky

caryatid shouldering still the organ
of speech, with its cigarette, and ogling

the scenes, breathtaking for their oblivion
of propriety, happening in the avian

bedroom, exposed to a passing party,
and resembling now a windswept palm tree,

now a jumble of numerals insane with their quest for timing,
now a line scrawled in haste and rhyming.

1995

[*109*]

After Us

After us, it is certainly not the flood,
and not drought either. In all likelihood, the climate
in the Kingdom of Justice, with its four seasons, will
be temperate, so that a choleric, a melancholic,
a sanguinic, and a phlegmatic could rule by turns
three months each. From the standpoint of an encyclopedia,
that's plenty. Although, no doubt, caprices
of atmospheric pressure or those of temperature
might confuse a reformer. Still, the god of commerce
only revels in a rising demand for tweeds,
English umbrellas, worsted topcoats. His most dreaded enemies
are darned stockings and patched-up trousers.
It would seem that the rain outside the window
advocates precisely this distinctly frugal
approach to the landscape—more generally to all creation.
But the Constitution doesn't mention rain.
There's not a single reference in the Constitution
to barometers or, for that matter, to anyone
who, perched on a stool, holding a ball of yarn,
like some muscular Alcibiades, passes the
night poring over a fashion magazine's dog-eared pages
in the anteroom of the Golden Age.

1994

A Tale

I

In walks the Emperor, dressed as Mars;
   his medals clink and sway.
The General Staff sports so many stars,
   it looks like the Milky Way.

The Emperor says, "I guess you guess
   what you are here for."
The generals rise and bark, "Oh yes,
   Sire! To start a war."

"Right," says the Emperor. "Our enemy
   is powerful, mean, and brash.
But we'll administer him such an enema
   his toilet won't need a flush.

"Move your artillery! Move your warships!
   Where is my gorgeous horse?
Forward! May God, whom our nation worships,
   join our brave air force!"

"Yes!" cry the warriors. "Our job is carnage,
   ruin, destruction, void.
We promise, Sire: we'll find a Carthage
   and we'll leave it destroyed."

"Great!" cries the Emperor. "What one conquers
　　is up to the scholars' quills.
And let the Treasury boys go bonkers
　　trying to pay the bills."

The generals thunder: "Well said, Sire.
　　Our coin is of tolling bells.
May the sun that won't set over your empire
　　rise for nobody else!"

And off roars the turbine, off clangs the metal,
　　off they march, hand on hilt,
as many a rose curls its tender petal
　　ready to wait and wilt.

II

It's no Armageddon, it's not some smarmy
　　earthquake or H-bomb test.
No, it's just the Imperial Army
　　trying to do its best.

The sky is falling, the earth is gaping,
　　the ocean simply boils.
"Life," says the Emperor, "is just aping
　　popular abstract oils.

"War," he continues, "is like a museum."
   And the Top Brass agree:
"Sire, we'll paint like that ad nauseam,
   since Art equals History!

"History never says it's sorry,
   nor does it say, What if.
To enter History, a territory
   first has to come to grief."

"History never says it's sorry,"
   join the enlisted men.
"Who needs memento when we've got mori?
   History must know when."

"Ah, tell them to turn the good old horizon
   vertical, save its sail,"
adds the Emperor, with his eyes on
   the most minute detail.

"Yes," cry the generals. "Yes, for heaven's
   sake. That's what's been amiss.
Let's push the button and see what happens.
   This must be a masterpiece."

And lo, the world turns topsy-turvy,
   in other words, goes bust.
"Gosh," says the Emperor. "That was nervy,
   but, in the context, just."

                        III

Now there's nothing around to argue
   over: no pros or cons.
"Hey, enemy!" the Emperor shouts. "Are you
   there?" —There's no response.

Now it's pure space, devoid of mountains,
   plains, and their bric-a-brac.
"Let's," says the Emperor, "sing our anthem's
   lyrics and raise the flag."

Up flies the pennant, attended only
   by two or three evening bats.
"A victory often makes one lonely,"
   the Emperor says, then adds:

"Let's have a monument, since my stallion,
   white as a hyacinth,
is old and looks, as it were, quite alien;
   and write on the granite plinth:

" 'Tight was the enemy's precious anus.
    We, though, stood strong and firm.'
The critics might say that we went bananas.
    But we've got it all on film.

"Lest her sweet mutants still cry, the mother
    may sing them the ancient lay.
The future as such has no purpose, other
    than pushing down Replay."

At sunset, everything looks quite pretty.
    Down goes the temperature.
The world lies motionless, like a treaty
    without a signature.

The stars start to twinkle, remote and jolly.
    The eye travels rather far.
One feels a little bit melancholy.
    But there is one's cigar.

1995

Ode to Concrete

You'll outlast me, good old concrete,
as I've outlasted, it seems, some men
who had taken me, too, for a kind of street,
citing color of eyes, or mien.

So I praise your inanimate, porous looks
not out of envy but as the next
of kin—less durable, plagued with loose
joints, though still grateful to the architects.

I applaud your humble—to be exact,
meaningless—origins, roar and screech,
fully matched, however, by the abstract
destination, beyond my reach.

It's not that nothing begets its kind
but that the future prefers to court
a date that's resolutely blind
and wrapped in a petrified long skirt.

1995

At the City Dump
in Nantucket

To Stephen White

The perishable devours the perishable in broad daylight,
moribund in its turn in late November:
the seagulls, trashing the dump, are trying to outnumber
the snow, or have it at least delayed.

The reckless primordial alphabet, savaging every which
way the oxygen wall, constitutes a preface
to the anarchy of the refuse:
in the beginning, there was a screech.

In their stammering Ws one reads not hunger but
the prurience of comma-sharp talons toward
what outlasts them, or else a torn-out
page's flight from the volume's fat,

while some mad anemometer giddily spins its cups
like a haywire tea ceremony, and the Atlantic
is breasting grimly with its athletic
swells the darkening overcast.

1995–96

A Photograph

We lived in a city tinted the color of frozen vodka.
Electricity arrived from afar, from swamps,
and the apartment, at evening, seemed
smudged with peat and mosquito-bitten.
Clothes were cumbersome, betraying
the proximity of the Arctic. At the corridor's farthest end
the telephone rattled, reluctantly coming back
to its senses after the recently finished war.
The three-ruble note sported coal miners and aviators.
I didn't know that someday all this would be no more.
In the kitchen, enameled pots
were instilling confidence in tomorrow
by turning stubbornly, in a dream, into headgear or
a Martian army. Motorcars also were
rolling toward the future and were mostly black,
gray, and sometimes—the taxis—
even light brown. It's strange and not very pleasant
to think that even metal knows not its fate
and that life has been spent for the sake of an apotheosis
of the Kodak company, with its faith in prints
and jettisoning of the negatives.
Birds of Paradise sing, despite no bouncing branches.

1994

[*118*]

A Postcard

The country is so populous that polygamists and serial
killers get off scot-free and airplane crashes
are reported (usually on the evening news) only when they occur
in a wooded area—the difficulty of access
is most grievous if it's tinged with feelings for the environment.
Theaters are packed, both stalls and stage.
An aria is never sung by a single tenor:
normally they use six at once, or one that's as fat as six.
And the same goes for the government, whose offices stay lit up
through the night, working in shifts, like factories,
hostage to the census. Everything is pandemic.
What is loved by one is loved by many,
be it an athlete, a perfume, or bouillabaisse.
Therefore, no matter what you say or do *is* loyal.
Nature too seems to have taken note of the common denominator,
and whenever it rains, which is seldom, clouds linger longest over
not the army and navy stadium but the cemetery.

1994

Reveille

Birds acquaint themselves with leaves.
Hired hands roll up their sleeves.
In a brick malodorous dorm
boys awake awash in sperm.

Clouds of patently absurd
but endearing shapes assert
the resemblance of their lot
to a cumulative thought.

As the sun displays its badge
to the guilty world at large,
scruffy masses have to rise,
unless ordered otherwise.

Now let's see what one can't see
elsewhere in the galaxy:
life on earth, of which its press
makes a lot and comets less.

As a picture doomed to sneak
previews only, it's unique
even though some action must
leave its audience aghast.

Still, the surplus of the blue
up on high supplies a clue

as to why our moral laws
won't receive their due applause.

What we used to blame on gods
now gets chalked up to the odds
of small particles whose sum
makes you miss the older sham.

Yet regardless of the cause,
or effects that make one pause,
one is glad that one has been
caught this morning in between.

Painted by a gentle dawn
one is proud that like one's own
planet now one will not wince
at what one is facing, since

putting up with nothing whose
company we cannot lose
hardens rocks and—rather fast—
hearts as well. But rocks will last.

1996

Blues

Eighteen years I've spent in Manhattan.
The landlord was good, but he turned bad.
A scumbag, actually. Man, I hate him.
Money is green, but it flows like blood.

I guess I've got to move across the river.
New Jersey beckons with its sulphur glow.
Say, numbered years are a lesser evil.
Money is green, but it doesn't grow.

I'll take away my furniture, my old sofa.
But what should I do with my windows' view?
I feel like I've been married to it, or something.
Money is green, but it makes you blue.

A body on the whole knows where it's going.
I guess it's one's soul that makes one pray,
even though above it's just a Boeing.
Money is green, and I am gray.

1992

At a Lecture

Since mistakes are inevitable, I can easily be taken
for a man standing before you in this room filled
with yourselves. Yet in about one hour
this will be corrected, at your and at my expense,
and the place will be reclaimed by elemental particles
free from the rigidity of a particular human shape
or type of assembly. Some particles are still free. It's not all dust.

So my unwillingness to admit it's I
facing you now, or the other way around,
has less to do with my modesty or solipsism
than with my respect for the premises' instant future,
for those aforementioned free-floating particles
settling upon the shining surface
of my brain. Inaccessible to a wet cloth eager to wipe them off.

The most interesting thing about emptiness
is that it is preceded by fullness.
The first to understand this were, I believe, the Greek
gods, whose forte indeed was absence.
Regard, then, yourselves as rehearsing perhaps for the divine encore,
with me playing obviously to the gallery.
We all act out of vanity. But I am in a hurry.

Once you know the future, you can make it come
earlier. The way it's done by statues or by one's furniture.

Self-effacement is not a virtue
but a necessity, recognized most often
toward evening. Though numerically it is easier
not to be me than not to be you. As the swan confessed
to the lake: I don't like myself. But you are welcome to my reflection.

1994

In Memory of
Clifford Brown

It's not the color blue, it's the color cold.
It's the Atlantic's color you've got no eyes for
in the middle of February. And though you sport a coat,
you're flat on your naked back upon the ice floe.

It's not a regular ice floe, meltdown-prone.
It's an argument that all warmth is foreign.
It's alone in the ocean, and you're on it alone,
and the trumpet's song is like mercury falling.

It's not a guileless tune that chafes in the darkness, though;
it's the gloveless, frozen to C-sharp fingers.
And a glistening drop soars to the zenith, so
as to glance at the space with no retina's interference.

It's not a simple space, it's a nothing, with
alts attaining in height what they lose in color,
while a spotlight is drifting into the wings,
aping the ice floe and waxing polar.

1993

Love Song

If you were drowning, I'd come to the rescue,
    wrap you in my blanket and pour hot tea.
If I were a sheriff, I'd arrest you
    and keep you in a cell under lock and key.

If you were a bird, I'd cut a record
    and listen all night long to your high-pitched trill.
If I were a sergeant, you'd be my recruit,
    and boy, I can assure you, you'd love the drill.

If you were Chinese, I'd learn the language,
    burn a lot of incense, wear funny clothes.
If you were a mirror, I'd storm the Ladies',
    give you my red lipstick, and puff your nose.

If you loved volcanoes, I'd be lava,
    relentlessly erupting from my hidden source.
And if you were my wife, I'd be your lover,
    because the Church is firmly against divorce.

1995

To My Daughter

Give me another life, and I'll be singing
in Caffè Rafaella. Or simply sitting
there. Or standing there, as furniture in the corner,
in case that life is a bit less generous than the former.

Yet partly because no century from now on will ever manage
without caffeine or jazz, I'll sustain this damage,
and through my cracks and pores, varnish and dust all over,
observe you, in twenty years, in your full flower.

On the whole, bear in mind that I'll be around. Or rather,
that an inanimate object might be your father,
especially if the objects are older than you, or larger.
So keep an eye on them always, for they no doubt will judge you.

Love those things anyway, encounter or no encounter.
Besides, you may still remember a silhouette, a contour,
while I'll lose even that, along with the other luggage.
Hence, these somewhat wooden lines in our common language.

1994

Flourish

O if the birds sang while the clouds felt bored by singing,
and the eye gaining blue as it traced their trill
could make out the keys in the door and, beyond, a ceiling,
and those whose address at present begins with nil.

And other than that, it's just shifting of chairs and sofas,
and flowers on walls and in vases obstruct their view.
And if there was ever a bee sans beehive or solace
with extra spores on its paws, it's you.

O if the transparent things in their blue garret
could hold their eye-dodging matter in second gear
to curdle themselves one day into a tear or star at
this end of the universe. Afterwards, everywhere.

Yet oxygen seems to be just the raw material
for lace strung out on spokes in the tsars' back yard,
and the statues freeze as though they smell a serial
Decembrist, beheaded later and breathing hard.

1994

MCMXCIV

Lousy times: nothing to steal and no one to steal from.
The legions return empty-handed from their faraway expeditions.
A sibyl confuses the past with the future as if she were a tree.
And actors whom nobody now applauds
forget the great lines. Forgetting, however, is the mother
of classics. Eventually these years
too will be seen as a slab of marble
with a network of capillaries (the aqueduct, the system
of taxation, the catacombs, the gossip),
with a tuft of grass bursting up from within its crack.
Whereas this was a time of poverty and of boredom,
when there was nothing to steal, still less to buy,
not to mention to offer somebody as a present.
The fault was not Caesar's, more suffering than the rest
because of the absence of luxury. Nor should one blame the stars,
since the low overcast relieves the planets of responsibility
toward the settled terrain: an absence
cannot influence a presence. And here's precisely where
a marble slab starts, because one-sidedness
is the enemy of perspective. Perhaps it's simply
that things, more quickly than men, have lost
their desire to multiply. In this white captivity.

1994

MCMXCV

The clowns are demolishing the circus. The elephants have run
off to India;
tigers sell, on the sidewalk, their stripes and hoops;
under the leaky cupola, there is hanging, off the trapeze,
as in a wardrobe, the limp tuxedo
of a disillusioned magician;
and little horses, casting off their embroidered blankets, pose
for a portrait of the new engine. In the arena,
knee-deep in sawdust, clowns, wildly wielding
sledgehammers, demolish the circus.
The public is either absent or doesn't clap.
Only a miniature shaggy poodle
still yelps incessantly, feeling she's getting closer
to her sugar lump: feeling that any second
she'll be hitting nineteen ninety-five.

1995

View with a Flood

A somewhat familiar landscape, currently flooded. Currently
it's only cupolas, spires, treetops, a rainy gauze.
The throat wells up with a gurgling, passionate commentary,
but out of the bunch of words all that remains is was.

That's how, toward the end, a mirror reflects a veteran's
baldness, but not his face, let alone his butt.
Below, sheer washed-out scribblings and swallowed utterance.
Above, the snatch of a cloud. And you stand in water. Cut.

It seems the scene is somewhere in the Netherlands; very probably
prior to their having dikes, and names like Van Dam, De Vries.
Or else it's Southeast Asia, with the monsoon soberly
softening up the paddies. But you are no rice.

Clearly it rose drop by drop, for years, attempting a neverscape
whose potable swells now crave new distances: salty, vast.
And it's high time to shoulder the child like a periscope
to spot the faraway enemy battleships steaming fast.

1993

Taps

I've been reproached for everything save the weather
and in turn my own neck was seeking a scimitar.
But soon, I'm told, I'll lose my epaulets altogether
and dwindle into a little star.

I'll twinkle among the wires, a sky's lieutenant,
and hide in clouds when thunder roars,
blind to the troops as they fold their pennant
and run, pursued by the pen, in droves.

With nothing around to care for, it's of no import
if you are blitzed, encircled, reduced to nil.
Thus wetting his dream with the tumbled ink pot,
a schoolboy can multiply as no tables will.

And although the speed of light can't in nature covet
thanks, non-being's blue armor plate,
prizing attempts at making a sifter of it,
might use my pinhole, at any rate.

1994